How To Get Loans For A

Black Business

With Bad Credit

REAL LIFE SITUATIONS

BY SEJJ JACKSON

A URBAN RAPPORT BOOK

This publication is designed to provide competent and reliable information regarding the subject matter covered. However, it is sold with the understanding that the author and publishers are not engaged in rendering legal, financial, or other professional advice. Laws and practices often vary from state to state and if legal or other expert assistance is required, the services of a professional should be sought. The author and publishers specifically disclaim any liability that is incurred from the use or application of the contents of this book.

No part of this publication may be reproduced, stored in a retrieval system, or transmitted, in any form or by any means, electronic, mechanical, photocopying, recording, or otherwise, without the prior written permission of the publisher. Printed in the United States of America.

Copyright © 2016 by The Urban Rapport all rights reserved.

www.theurbanrapport.com

ISBN: 978-1537726458

Printed in the United States of America

First Edition

This book is dedicated to every aspiring entrepreneur, and my mother MS. Tiffany Ivory, love u much!

- SEJJ JACKSON

How to Get Loans For A
Black Business With Bad Credit

REAL-LIFE SITUATIONS

BY SEJJ JACKSON

A Urban Rapport Book

Table Of Contents

Introduction..8

Chapter One...20
Banking Black In America

Chapter Two...27
The Approach To Obtaining Financing

Chapter Three...34
Hard Money

Chapter Four...51
Revenue Based Funding

Chapter Five..57
Angel Investors

Chapter Six..65
Venture Capital

Chapter Seven...70
Initial Public Offering

Chapter Eight..83
Direct Public Offering

Chapter Nine...94
Crowd Based Funding

Conclusion...101
Acknowledgements....................................104
About The Author.....................................108

Introduction

Introduction

"So You Need Financing But Can't Get It From The Bank"

The commercial financing industry is rigorous and specialized. Whether you're an established business or thinking about starting one, at some point, funding will be needed. The process for obtaining a commercial loan is hard even if you're an established business, nonetheless a business still in the conceptional phase. With that being so, the entire funding process can be even more troublesome for a black business. Most African Americans will not meet the harsh banking requirements. As an African American, this can make the funding process seem frustrating and discouraging.

Often, lending institutions unintentionally make it harder for African Americans to be approved for business loans. By implementing (risk management) lending criteria that favor those with certain resources readily available to them. Like cosigners, cash, equity, or tangible assets that can be easily liquidated. The majority of black business owners do not have access to these resources that will be needed for a traditional loan approval. With numerous banking requirements that will have to be met, this will cause many African Americans to be denied a traditional loan. For example, you may have an excellent credit score but not meet the bank's income requirement. Or you might meet the bank's income requirement, but not have the proper debt to income ratio to be approved. Many black business owners may never be able to meet all of the tough traditional loan requirements, therefore never receiving funding. This creates the need for alternative financing.

In this book, I explore many alternative financing channels that have been proven to work for African Americans. Despite the funding challenges, you'll be able to find an alternative funding avenue that works for you. And I cover the most proven ones here.

If you're like the majority of small business owners, or you are considering opening a business, obtaining funding is a critical step. However, it may seem like getting approval for a loan is impossible. Statistics show that some 85% of companies require funding at some point during their existence. A little less than 15% actually get some form of traditional financing. This leaves a staggering 70% of business out in the cold. These statistics are not based on race or ethnicity. So you can imagine how many black business are denied within these figures.

The government insists that small businesses are the backbone of the economy but have yet to approve laws that would make access to capital attainable. We understand the probability of getting a loan approval is minimal. So what's a Black business owner to do? Let's explore a few alternative methods:

1. Hard Money

Hard Money is precisely what the name states, hard money. These are loans that carry a high-interest rate along with a short term. These loans are designed for those who need funding but cannot get it from banks. Most of the hard money loans are asset based, meaning the lender's criteria is based on assets like inventory, real property, or any other equipment that has value.

2. Revenue Based Lending

Revenue based lenders are similar to hard money lenders, but instead of being based on assets, revenue based lenders make their lending decision on company's annual revenue. Revenue based lenders tend to have more money than hard money lenders. Most hard money lenders are individuals that are trying to diversify their funds by offering loans at higher than normal interest rates. Hard money lenders have a lending thresholds that they are comfortable staying within. While revenue based lenders will handle larger than usual loan amounts. The interest rates might be slightly higher than a hard money loan, but you typically get funding faster.

3. Angel Investors

   Angel investors are investment funds ran by an individual with the sole purpose of investing in businesses that meet the fund's lending criteria. Every angel fund has its lending criteria, but most angels are cause driven. Angels tend to be more emotion driven and cause based. Angel funds are run by individuals with exceptional business know how. Instead of charging an interest rate, Angels look to acquire equity and become a partner in business.

4. Venture Capital

   Venture capital is where the big dogs play. These are professionally run investment funds with the sole intention of making money fast as possible. They don't care about cash or credit. What they are looking for is growing revenue, profit, and good business margins. If they see your business as a money making machine, then they'll give you enough money to a growing business. But this comes at a cost to you by way of ownership in your company. You will have to give up large portions of ownership in exchange for VC funds. I will go more into depth on this in the venture capitalist chapter.

5. Initial Public Offering

This method is better known as an IPO and is the route to make a private company public. IPOs are handled by broker-dealers that sell shares of businesses to the general public. Broker-dealers handle this process from start to finish. Even though this is one of the most expensive ways to obtain financing, this method by far is the best route to take when needed ongoing financing. Because you will always have access to the capital, you need by offering more shares to the general public. There are some major pitfalls with going this route. I will cover those pitfalls in the chapter titled IPOs.

6. Direct Public Offerings

Direct public offerings, (DPOs) is an alternative form of an IPO. This is where you become the broker-dealer for your own company. The main difference between an IPO and a DPO is DPOs cannot sell equities to the general public, you'll have to sell them to accredited investors. However, with a proper ran DPO funding round, you'll be able to raise an unlimited amount of money. But going this route comes are a steep price. DPOs happen to be the most expensive route to take by far, but it has the best results when trying to maintain control. Because a broker-dealer isn't involved, means you'll have to cover all the cost of running a DPO yourself. With the added cost and responsibility there are huge benefits to this channel of financing. I will cover them all in the chapter titled Direct Public Offerings.

7. Crowd Based Funding

Crowd-based funding is something that's been around for less than 10 years. This is where everyday people can invest in your company for a dollar at a time. Crowd Based Funding is a good funding route for a company still in the seed phase. I'll go more in depth in the crowd based funding chapter.

The private sector is left to fend for itself when it comes to securing financing. So don't feel alone, where there's a will there's away, and I'm going to show you the way right here in this book. These are financing channels I have experience with. So learn and take from my experience of seeking alternative financing.

Chapter One

Banking Black In America

"Where there is no struggle, there is no strength." – Oprah Winfrey

It's already hard enough being a business owner in America. That title comes with its own basic challenges. But those challenges of a non-African American business owner are intensified ten fold for an African American business owner, because of the typical stereotype of an African American out the gate. So what seems easy for most businesses, can very well be harder for black businesses because of the stereotype that's dawned upon them. This stereotype can affect you in other areas of business like with vendors. So when people make the statement about having the same challenges as a black business owner, I beg to differ. African American business owners have to fight the typical stereotype every day.

Nowadays, People will prejudge you before laying eyes on you. This feeds into the stereotype that African Americans have to fight every day. Often, people will hear your voice and rush to a quick conclusion about you that may not be true, when you're an African American. Then they'll be then you handle you based on that wrong perception. So the opportunities afforded a black business owner are less, while his challenges are more. This wrong stereotype has a direct impact on our banking system here in America. Yes, you hear about banks being an opportunity lender, but I can show you exactly how they get around that "motto." Because that's exactly what that is, just a motto.

But to show some justice towards the banking system here in America we have to look at the history if the system from the beginning.

Not to dwell too much on history, you have to remember where the banking system comes from to understand why it operates the way it does. The banking and justice systems of American, came from Great Britain when they settled Jamestown in the 1700's. The banking system was more of a bartering system at first. People could use chickens, horses, cows whatever they had. So if you wanted a loan, you would have to bring in your goods for the bank to hold until the debts been paid. The banking system quickly changed after the Revolutionary War. Now you had people with land that needed loans for farming. Knowing most people didn't have enough resources to collateralize large bank loans, sharecropping was introduced. This allowed farmers to get a loan based on their crops. But at this time African Americans were not considered people, but only property. So legally African Americans couldn't own assets. It was illegal for a black man to grow a crop and call it his own. This formed the basis of the entire banking system that's still running today.

The American banking system was not created or designed with African-Americans in mind. The culture of the original banking system is still in effect today. Little has changed behind closed doors, as far as the culture is concerned. So you're forced to bank with a system that didn't recognize you as a human being. Back then it was against the law for an African American to get any loans. To my amazement, a lot of the original banking laws are still on the books. Don't believe me, look at the Alabama Constitution. This systematic oppressive banking culture has transcended into all aspects of banking including the credit scoring system which is the enforcer of this unfavorable banking culture.

This is something people don't talk about, but a conversation needs to be had for things to change.

Because the average African American has multiple banking responsibilities like retirement, mortgages, car loans, school loans we have to do business with traditional lending institutions. Yes, there are Black banks, but guess what? They are still apart of the same oppressive banking culture. Have you ever noticed banks that claim to serve the black community, will also have the same rules as the bank down the street? Because they are all part of the same banking culture and system. So just because they have the title as a black bank does not make a difference at all.

One thing you have to remember when dealing with these banks is how they see you. And I'm not saying this in a way to put African Americans down or be negative at all, I'm just real. What you see in the mirror is exactly what the bankers see. This reality forces you to have to exhibit Superman like confidence to get what you're looking for. What I mean is you have to act like you already own a multimillion dollar business even though you're depositing a $100 check. People like doing business with confident people. Studies have shown that people feel comfortable, and better about themselves when they deal with confident people. You have to learn how to present yourself as someone who doesn't need money to get it. If a bank sees you as somebody, then they will treat you like somebody. If they feel like you are someone of importance, then banks will do everything that can get your business.

Another tip is to always deal with upper-level management. If you cannot get to a vice president, then don't do business with that bank. You get more perks and avoid headaches by doing business straight with the bank's management. I've had a loan turned down in the bank's lobby but then get approved by a vice president a few weeks later. Seriously, the bank turned me down when I applied for a loan. Then 6 weeks later, I had a card in my mailbox with double the credit limit that I was seeking. So it doesn't matter how much money you have, make sure you deal with a vice president. VP's will be happy to do business with you because they get huge incentives for new business. So if the vice president feels like you're somebody(exert that level of confidence I talked about), then they will give you special privileges that others might not get

Chapter Two
The Approach To Obtaining Financing

"Thou shalt not forget that money is only money and not character or fame." — Steven J. Lee

You need to have a positive approach when looking for funding. Having a positive outlook will keep your stress level down and help you focus on your overall goal which is to get money.

Hunting for money is a very stressful process and can dampen your life if you let it. You will often find it hard to sleep or find yourself working more hours without immediate results. Not having immediate results will make a lot of people close their business faster because they feel like they'll never get the money they need. But you have to remember that the work you put in now will show up later.

The good thing about the financing journey is that once you've been down this road, the next time you need funding the journey becomes easier. And the key is to remain active and positive about each financing channel you take. Regardless if you get the money or not, it's always a numbers game. The more times you present your company to a financier the closer you come to getting the money you're seeking. So instead of paying attention to the negatives teach yourself to always stay positive. If you present your idea to 100 people, 1 is destined to say yes. And when you get that yes, the 99 who said no will be forgotten.

So remember always have a positive outlook while on this journey. Being positive is a therapeutic way to get past the no's. Obtaining financing isn't easy. It requires energy to keep going day after day, night after night. But having a positive mental state will make it easier. Your luck will change for the better.

But first and foremost, enjoy this journey!

Real Life Situation

Let me share a personal story about when I tried to take out a $50k loan from a CD I had set up just for that purpose.

I went to a real estate conference where they talked about ways to establish credit before needing it. The method was to open a CD at a small bank, leave it alone for a few months, then take out a loan against the CD, and just pay the interest on the loan, therefore, building a payment history. After three months, pay the loan off. This would build a positive credit score by having a large bank loan being paid off. But let me tell you what happen when I tried to do just that.

I started banking with a small bank. It was a bank that had just opened a branch close to my house, so it fit the small bank criteria I was looking for perfectly. I opened up several business accounts and started banking with them months before establishing the CD. I got so well known at the bank that I could just call in, and they would do whatever I needed them to do. By this time I had taken out the CD.

Well, I opened a $50k CD and continued banking with them on the regular. The bank was right down the street from my house, and I had to pass the bank on my way out of my neighborhood, so it convenient for me. I would often make large deposits, 5 and sometimes 6 figures checks. They never placed any holds on my funds, the money would be available immediately. Everything was good until I tried to take out a loan against my own CD. The bank declined me for a loan on my own money! The following week, I brought in $78k check. This wasn't nothing out the ordinary for me. All of a sudden, they wanted to put a 21-day hold on the check. The money was from an attorney's office from a closing I had, plus it was made off a local bank. So there weren't any issues with the check. Now I deposited two 6-figure checks the prior month with no issues at all. So right there I knew what it was.

I was highly upset and mad. I just didn't understand what was going on. The assistant manager told me that they were making some drastic changes, winking at me. Now I understood where the assistant manager was coming from, and she was always the most helpful person at the branch. It took me months to come to the realization that me being African American had something to do with this. Because soon after that, they started to really give cause me some issues. It seemed as if they wanted to run me off, and they manage to do just that.

I ended up going to another bank, but that stuck with me for a while. Having been denied a loan against my own money made me look at things differently. Being declined that one time helped me because I made sure I wasn't caught in a situation where I needed a bank again. I became my own bank and lent money to myself. My money that I had a place away just in case I needed money to flip a house or just to run my business came in handy in the long run.

So keep this in mind, it doesn't matter how much money you have, they will still treat you a certain way just because of your African American. So make sure you create a situation where you don't need a bank. But that's easier said than done right?

Well, let's talk about other financing channels to get money for your business.

Chapter Three
Hard Money
The Bank Has Told You NO! No worries.

Hard money lenders are lenders that have very high-interest rates with low terms. The interest rates can be as high as 50%. Hard money loans are administered by individuals who are seeking higher returns on their money than what traditional banks are offering. Hard money loans tend to have very lax lending requirements. And most are asset based if you're purchasing inventory or real estate. Most hard money lenders want skin in the game meaning some form of collateral. The collateral can be cash, inventory, equity, or an asset that can be easily liquidated. The loan terms can range from 6-18 months in most cases to 3 years depending on the loan amount.

Hard Money lenders are private and like to do business fast. So if you're planning on using hard money lenders, make sure all your paperwork is in order. Having your ducks in a row is critical when trying to get a hard money loan because hard money lenders don't have massive amounts of money laying around. They recycle their loans quick as possible. So there won't be a lot of time for you to gather stuff together. Someone might get the funding you were seeking all because you didn't have your stuff in order. Keep your business in order so when a hard money lender asks you for something you'll have it ready.

Things that you will need to have in order:

1. Get Your Organization Together.

    This mean if you're going to incorporate, make sure this is done before you start approaching lenders. If you're running your business as a sole proprietor, it's less likely you'll get funding. Getting your business organized isn't hard at all. If you're a member of theurbanrapport.com, we have several tools for you to incorporate your business right from home. Takes about one day depending on where you live in the country.

2. Have Your Tax Information Together.

You will need to have your personal and business tax information together. Have your last three years tax information handy. It doesn't matter if you're showing losses on your taxes. Lenders need to see the money you're reporting to the IRS. No better way to accomplish this than looking at some taxes.

Also, make sure you have you EIN letter handy. If you don't have one, go to the IRS website and get one. When you visit the website, make sure you print or save the EIN number as a PDF for your records.

3. Get A Professional Business Plan.

You will need a professional business plan. And I'm not talking about something somebody rushed to complete in between going to classes. I'm talking about a professional business plan with researched information, and accurate projections. People tend to short change themselves with having a great business plan. Most people just come up with a business idea, and go forward, without a plan on paper. Not having a business plan diminishes your chance of succeeding by almost 75%. Putting an adequate business plan together forces you to think about every aspect of your business in detail. Having a business plan is one of the main difference between running a real business and just having a hobby.

You'll need a professional business plan because it'll speak the language of the lender. What do I mean by "language of the lender?" You'll have to remember that these are professional business men and women. They have a certain degree of business success that has afforded them the opportunity to invest in other businesses. So these leaders know what they are doing. You will have to speak their language to get financing. The lender will need to understand you, your business, what you're trying to accomplish. Having a professional business plan will allow the lender to interpret your thoughts and ideas in a technical term, which he understands. Many loans are declined solely because the lender didn't understand the person or business. Being able to communicate effectively with a lender is your most valuable weapon in your arsenal. Use it!

4. You Need A Good Synopsis or Summary.

A good synopsis can be read in about 60-90 sec. People tend to make their lending decisions in 60-90 sec. Therefore, the synopsis can make or break the deal in less than 2 mins. But what is a synopsis or summary? This is a technical document showcasing a need. What are you financing? For what? And how will that funding help you? What interest rates and terms are you looking for and why? How are the lenders going to get their money back? How long will it take? All these questions will need to be answered in a synopsis. Whoever's doing your business plan should also do you professional synopsis too. Remember because the synopsis needs to speak the technical language that the lender understands along with the business plan. So I highly advise that you hire a professional to prepare your business documents. If you don't know where to start then join theurbanrapport.com where we have numerous professionals ready to help you, some even for free.

5. Branding.

Lenders like to do business with people they see as business savvy. This means having your businesses branding message down pact. You'll need your message on as many things as possible like pens, cups, stationary, and cards. When you do present your information to a lender, they'll see your company's message. This goes back to what I was talking about with speaking the language of the lender. Lenders understand a technical businesses message. And your business needs to speak that message with every chance it gets. This is vital when trying to initiate a banking relationship with a hard money lender. The first impression needs to the best.

Hard Money is easy to get, but it comes with a cost. You might get a 30% interest rate with a six-month term. After the 6 months is up, you'll have to pay the loan back plus the 30%. Nowadays, many hard money lenders payment schedules can be weekly to ensure they get their money back.

When dealing with hard money, make sure you can afford the cost of the money too. Add this to your business plan's financial projections so everything will be on paper. Make sure you stick to that plan only adjusting it when you need to. In other words, prepare diligently before you get this money. So when you do get it, you'll already have a plan in place for use of the money.

"When money realizes that it is in good hands, it wants to stay and multiply in those hands."
― Idowu Koyenikan

Real Life Situation

I'm going to tell you two situations that I've experienced while dealing with hard money lenders. I'm telling you these stories so that you can pull information from them that will help you with your journey. So take from these stories at will.

I was a young guy about 18 or 19 years of age flipping three to four houses a week. I could purchase, rehab, and sell a home within 45 days. I built a system, and all I had to do was feed the system money.

Having a strong relationship with a hard money lender was the reason I was able to do so much. The hard money lender was an older Jewish guy that needed a reason to get out the house. So he lent several guys money to flip homes. The guy had deep pockets and could lend larger loan amounts than anybody else around outside a bank. His lending decisions were based solely on the property. So if I ran across a home I knew he would like, I would immediately lock the house under contract because I knew he would give me the money.

But there were some things about this guy that made it difficult to work with him sometimes. The main issue was that he'll get emotionally involved. Often, I would get a house knowing that he would lend the money. But when it came time for him to close the deal, he'll have to be sold on the house because he allowed his emotions to get involved. After about 15mins of back and forth he would always come around, though, but at times the situation would get stressful. So I took on two other hard money lenders in addition to him. So I always had three ways to get funding within a few days if I needed money.

With all three of hard money lenders, I knew exactly how each liked to work. I so was able to complete projects without any of my personal money, by building relationships with these guys. They knew I was consistent and worked harder than anybody else. So they gradually got to the point of trusting me enough to take over their abandoned projects. These projects stemmed from bad loans they made to guys that were in over their heads, and these investors would just walk away from a project. The lenders would hand me these projects interest-free! These were the same guys that had charged me an arm and leg at first, but now they were basically giving me money.

So you need to establish a good solid relationship with your hard money lender. They might charge you out the ass the first couple times around, but in due time they'll start giving you benefits that others don't get. So when you're in business, you need partners that have your back like. And hard money lenders tend to be the best types of partners to have.

Second Story

The second story is about my primary hard money lender I talked about in story one. There are many benefits when dealing with hard money lenders, and I pointed them out in story one. But some downsides come with hard money too.

I ran into a raggedy old dingy house in the middle of a prominent neighborhood. This community happens to be the same neighborhood that my primary hard money lender lives in. So I knew he would lend on the house. But I sat back on the deal for a couple of weeks because I knew I would have a different approach since I would be asking for four times as much as he would usually lend me.

See I know one law stands to be true when you're dealing with someone with a greedy person. The rush of making more money tends to be a greedy person's addiction. And my primary hard money lender was very greedy. It's just like a drug that's no different from the excitement of gambling. And I knew if I were to present him with a house around the corner from his, where a quick $250k could be made, that greed would show up. So I came up with a plan.

I put together a package of about ten homes that I wanted to do all at the same time. My other hard money lenders didn't have that kind of money to lend. So I made a call to my primary hard money guy pitching him on the house down the street from his, he immediately got excited. I mean this neighborhood was the top of the top...this and that... so he had to see about this opportunity. We met up at the house, walked around it for a minute. While looking at the house, I noticed he hadn't said too much. When I got through pitching him on the deal, he just said that he'll get back to me on it. I knew I had him.

He was quiet for a reason, and I'm about to tell you why in just a second. After a few weeks of him saying nothing about the deal, I ran by the house and noticed that the house had been sold. So I asked him about the house, and he admitted that he bought and sold it. I knew he was going to undercut me and buy the home for himself. That's why I put together a ten house package before I approached him with the deal. So when he did undercut me, he would feel so bad that he'll fund whatever I wanted. And that's exactly what he did, and I made almost double of what I would've made on that one house.

So you have to vigilant and watch your back when dealing with hard money lenders. Because they can be slick and you'll end up in a bind all because you don't know what you're doing. So make sure to take the time to read and understand all of your loan documents. Have someone who has experience dealing with hard money lenders take a look at them. Because trust me hard money lenders can be sharks.

You can find a list of hard money lenders at theurbanrapport.com. We update the list every month. It's a great resource to have on your financing journey.

Chapter Four
Revenue Based Loans

"Price ain't merely about numbers. It's a satisfying sacrifice." — Toba Beta

Revenue-based loans are loans that are based on credit card sales or gross annual income. These are nontraditional banks that base their lending criteria on gross revenue. These loans are indeed hard money loans but in a more traditional sense. You will have to fill out a traditional loan application called a 1003. This is the same application that traditional banks use. The only difference is that these revenue based lenders will only use your credit score to calculate your interest rates. Your credit doesn't affect your loan qualification at all. These rates will be as high as 40% with 6 to 18-month terms. The loan payments are made daily by small withdraws from your bank account. The loan approval amount will be up to 10% of your annual gross revenue, regardless of credit. If your business makes $12,500 per month in revenue (or $150,000 per year), then your loan will be $15,000. You can expect 5-7 business days to get funded.

Revenue-based loans are indeed short-term loans. Sometimes you can stretch the loan's term if you need more time, but this is not a solution for long-term financing. The interest rates are too high, and the loan is paid back by small daily withdraws from your bank account until the entire loan is paid back. This can put some financial stress on your business if you don't manage your funds right. So make sure you can afford revenue based loans before you apply for them. The way you do that is to take a look at your books now and add the additional cost of money along with the payment schedule.(I go more in depth at theurbanrapport.com) If you're in the red at any time during the loan's term, then this is not a good financing route for you. But if you're in the black during the loan's term, then this indicates your ability to bring in revenue during the course of the loan which is what you want.

I like these loans because once you pay the loan off, you'll be able to get a larger loan at a better rate. So this allows you to build up a line of credit that will end up being worth several hundred thousand dollars very quick. And when you're in business, a line of credit can be a lifesaver. So if you can afford to take this route, after looking at your books and adding in the extra cost of money, then take this route even if you don't need the money right away. So when you do need money, you'll have it.

These revenue based loans are spreading like a wildfire. They are coming up all over the place. Some of them offer better terms and interest rates than others. But they're criteria tends to be the same. Which is 3-12 months bank statements? This is all you'll need to be approved. They'll give you an approval amount based on your statements and interest rates will be based on your credit.

So all you need is 6 months of business banking statements (some lenders will ask you for 12 months), and an active business bank account. That's it! You'll have your money in about three days.

There's a lot of information on revenue based lenders at theurbanrapport.com. Make sure you join to get access.

Real Life Situations

For a whole year and a half, I kept getting offers from these revenue lending companies. At the time I didn't understand their model, and I didn't need money. So I gave them the cold shoulder until one day one of the companies belatedly sent me a check. Of course, I called the company, and they told me to cash it, its mines. Who sends $38k checks around! I felt like these folks were trying to make a fool of me. Finally, I decided to find out what these companies were all about and agreed to the loan.

I had $38k principle and $15k to pay back within 6mo. So I had to pay a total of $53k back in six months. They took 1.5% of the total amount from my bank account every day. I had to make sure I had enough money in that particular account to cover those daily payments. I ended up taking out a few more loans to get my line of credit up. Everything worked out fine.

So you never want to stigmatize lenders because you never know which one will end up being your best friend. And we all need best friends with a lot of money who's ready to lend. So if you choose to take this route, take full advantage of the opportunity. But only after deciding if you can afford the money.

Chapter Five
Angel Investors

"Business is still more often about whom you know, not what you know." —Alejandro Cremades

Angel investors are individuals who believe in providing opportunities to small businesses by investing in them. These people can be family or friends, but most likely you'll end up using one of the thousands of angel funds that are out there. Angel investors take more of a traditional approach to lending, minus the credit requirements. They lend based on the type of business you have, and the likelihood of you succeeding. Angel investors are professional investors with the accredited investor designation that the SEC requires for high-risk private investments. The interest rates and loan terms are more in line with banks.

Loans from angels can be either short or long term. Whatever you need an angel investor can cover it. Angels might require a percentage of your company because essentially they're equity seekers (Meaning they're looking for businesses that show promise of being successful). If you're a startup needing financing, angels are the route to go.

To get a loan from an angel investor, you will have to have a professional business plan made. Not only the business plan needs to be right, but your management team also. Most angels base their lending decisions on the management team's experience. Emotions sometimes can play a part in the financing decision as well. Angels will need to feel comfortable with lending you money. This is why you'll have to have everything in order before seeking funding from them. Because once the opportunity is gone, it's gone. And a lot of the time angels will want to review your business plan before even meeting you. The plan showcases your business savviness and shows them that you know what you're doing. There's a particular language these guys speak. And you're job is to find out what that language is so you'll be able to communicate with them in their language. This is how you increase your chances of getting the money you need.

The best way to accomplish this is by having your business plan professionally prepared by someone who's dealt with angel investors. You have to remember, these are very successful businesspeople. They know what they're doing, and they know what to look for. So if you don't communicate in a way that they understand, then you won't be getting any money period.

Angels are good for either long term or short term financing. Most of the time, all you have to do is get one angel on board and others will follow. Angels tend to share investments. Meaning if one thinks you're a good investment, then others will want to invest with you. Angel investors will tend to lend small portions of money. So if you're needed a few million, then this isn't the route for you. They'll end up only financing a portion of whatever you're asking for. So often you will still have to take on more investors after the first round with an angel. At this point, you can expect to give up some of those business shares you're sitting on. These types of investors are interested in the company as an investment, not just lending.

But one good thing about angels, they're with you all the way. So if you run into money issues later on after the first round of financing, they'll give you more. The bad side about this is you'll have to give up more of your company. And in some instances, I've seen an angel take ownership of a company because the entrepreneur wasn't making the projections in his business plan. And his business needed more money. For more money, he had to give up more shares. He gave up more than 50% of his business. But he got the money he needed, and the company ended up flourishing.

We have free materials at theurbanrapport.com, along with a list of angel investors. You can use these resources to put a plan together professionally.

Real-life Situations

I had a friend who went to college with me. My friend always has some business idea. The guy would come up with something so fast, but never had money behind him. Well, one day he was talking about his latest business idea in a bookstore. He got excited about all the possibilities that his business had all loud ambitions. Well someone was listening.

The gentleman came over introduced himself and started asking questions about his business. An hour later the gentleman invited him to pitch in front of some of his friends, the following day. These men happened to be some prominent angel investors. They gave him $6Million by the time he walked out that meeting. Today the pharmaceutical company is thriving. It ain't what you know, it's who you know.

They gave him the financing he needed, and then some to become 50% partners. This gave him the oxygen he needed to build the business into what it is today. I would tell you the company's name, but ain't nobody cutting me no endorsement checks. Lol

When you're dealing with this kind of investors, they're looking for your personal belief level. How much do you believe in yourself and your business? Your levels of belief should be so high only certain kinds of people will understand where you're coming from. Often, those are the ones that end up lending you money. Everybody else will call you crazy. But you'll need some level of craziness to go against the grain. My friend was a nut case! Always full of energy and ideas. But this goes to show you how enthusiastic he was about his business. Enthusiasm should be a moving feeling that comes over you every time you talk about your business. This is what make people believe in you, and your mission. So when you meet with any possible investor, remember always be positive, have your ducks in a row, and be over enthusiastic about your business at all times.

"Your every positive action in your life will increase your self-esteem and this self-esteem will boost you for more positive action to take you on success"
—Rashedur Ryan Rahman

Chapter Six
Venture Capital

"Fuck your feelings cause business is business; it's strictly financial." —Moosa Rahat

Venture Capitalist better know as VCs, are aggressive equity seekers. These are in fact investing funds that seek to acquire as much of equity as possible in a promising business. VC's plan to either take your company public or sell off their shares at a substantial profit as an exit strategy. Venture capitalist are looking to flip their money fast as possible. The world of venture capital is another world away from traditional financing. VC's are the largest financiers of businesses in the world. There are millions of VC funds out there. This route of funding is not for amateurs through. But if you have the right people, process, and product obtaining funding through this route can be much easier then trying a bank.(Learn More About The Three P's, people, process, and product at theurbanrapport.com)

A venture capital fund is run by a manager. The manager solicits accredited investors to invest in the fund, which then finds promising businesses to reinvest the money. The fund makes money from charging a percentage of all capital gains for the year. Investing in a VC fund is how most wealthy individuals spend their money. However, for you as the business owner who's looking for financing, this is a way to get millions. Unlike angels, VC's typically can have billions under their portfolio. VC's operate from either a high-interest rate (hard money) or equity. If you want funding from a VC, be ready to give up most of your business. The lending decision is solely based on you and your business and its potential to be successful. The requirements to even walk through a VC's door will require you to have a CPA and attorney handy. You will need a professional business plan prepared as well. We have many resources for free a theurbanrapport.com if you wish to take this route.

What you want to do is hire a consultant or securities attorney. They should know the ways of the VC world. Because dealing with VC's is a world of sharks you need the attorney to protect your business interest at all times. The attorney should be knowledgeable in all areas of the venture capital industry. You will need him during negotiations with a VC fund once you've found one. These people look strictly at your ability to make a profit. If you can't make that bottom line black, then this isn't for you because you'll end up losing your business.

This venture capital funding ties directly into having an "initial public offering" or IPOs (which we'll cover, in a later chapter). You'll need to have enough money to take on this channel of financing. It's not the most expensive, but it'll cost. Often, you'll have to travel to pitch your business to many different VCs around the country. If you happen to be somewhere close to Silicon Valley California, then you're lucky. But for most of us, we'll have to be on a plane for most of the time during your round of funding. Traveling like this can cost several thousands of dollars. Along with traveling you'll need a professional CPA and attorney to handle the back office business once you have a VC on the hook. These pros will have to step in to make sure everything is in compliance with local and federal investment laws to protect your business interest.

I would recommend you using some of the other methods of financing to get your business profitable before you take on a VC fund. Because you'll have to make sure you can handle the cost without delay. You'll need enough money to see the funding round through. The good part about this is that expenses can be reimbursed once you have funding in hand.

Real Life Situation

I had a VC out of New York that was going to fund my real estate sourcing company back in 2014. After spending $25k on just paperwork, and hiring the right personnel, the deal fell through. The VC wanted a higher percentage of my company than I was comfortable with. To me, they came off just wanting to make a quick dollar at the expensive of my business. So I backed out.

On this level of the game, you will learn that people don't really care about your company, you, or your product. All they care about is how fast they can make a profit. And if they can make a profit at your company's expense then they'll take full advantage of the opportunity. As a new company on the stock market that's the last thing you need is getting tied up in some bad business like that. You need someone that's there for the long haul and just not a quick profit. Once your company's stock hit that exchange, there's no going back to square one. You want your business to be in the best position possible out the gate. This might take some time to do, but it's well worth it. So take your time when dealing with VCs. Don't be so quick to jump at the first opportunity that presented.

Take your time to find out all the negatives involved. And to do this, you'll need a team of qualified professionals at your disposal.

If you decide on taking this route, make sure you have your attorney and CPA on deck at all times when dealing with VCs. All paperwork and communications should flow through your lawyer's desk. Don't make any decisions without that attorney. Make sure your attorney and CPA both have extensive experience with VCs.

Chapter Seven
Initial Public Offering

"If you never try, you'll never know, You are what you manifest." —Germany Kent

Initial public offerings (or IPOs) are investment offerings to the general public. These offerings are administered by investment broker-dealers. They packaged your deal and place your company shares on the stock market for the general public to purchase. This is an advanced method of getting funding for your business.

Now historically blacks weren't allowed to take part in stock offerings because we were considered animals and property. Animals and assets couldn't own anything by law. So, therefore, this system was also set up without the black man in mind.

But now that things have changed, they're still not enough African Americans taking part in wall street.

I think the lack of awareness plays a huge part in African Americans not taking part on wall street. It's more than just purchasing mutual funds. If we as black people were taught about wall street early on, then more African Americans would be producers on wall street today. Wall Street is where the real money is made. And to be a part of this club, you'll need the knowledge to dissect information that'll allow you to make money on the street (wall street that is). It's more to it than just producing an investment, and placing it on wall street. There are sharks every few feet on the street. And if you don't know how to navigate those treacherous waters, then you'll be swallowed up.

This is route is better taken after you've grown your company to a certain size in revenue. Once you've done that, then look at taking your company public. But let me tell you the truth. It will cost several hundred thousand dollars to do this. But all expenses can be reimbursed once funded.

IPOs are very cash intensive, meaning you'll have to afford this route. There are several expenses involved with taking a company public. You can very well except to spend $250-500k, over a period of two or more years. Before your stock hit the market, you'll need to drum up some awareness about your company. This promotional tour is called the dog and pony show. This is only one of many great expenses associated with going public.

(If you want more details, join theurbanrapport.com. We have detailed information for those wishing to go public. I have my personal brokerage firm with their contact information listed there also. They'll look at your deal, and give you insight on what you'll need to get listed)

The dog and pony show is a tour across the country to raise awareness of your shares going public. It consists of TV interviews, magazine interviews, etc. So imagine how much money this cost.

But before you even get to the dog and pony stage you'll have to negotiate with a brokerage firm first. Negotiating with a brokerage firm is a lot like negotiating with a venture capitalist. They want to see the money. But again, make sure you have an experienced attorney and CPA on staff, for the negotiations. Because just like a venture capitalist, broker-dealers will take advantage of you not knowing what you're doing. So investing in a good securities attorney and CPA is vital. They will protect you along the way, and give you advice when you need it.

Real Life Situations

I signed a broker-dealer agreement for my real estate sourcing company after my VC deal fell through. First I went the DPO or direct public offering route. After going through the DPO(Direct Public Offering) realms, I decided I no longer had the time to invest entirely towards that. I had two other companies to run, so I decided to go straight to the horse.

After months of seeking and negotiating with brokers, I finally inked a deal that'll take the company public late 2017, early 2018 if all goes right.

This is my first time taking a company public. So I had to learn the ropes quick. But I found that when you're black, brokers-dealers tend to not take you seriously. You have to build a track record on Wall Street first. Like seriously, you can have millions of dollars in the bank, and it still won't matter. Primarily, because most of these people also have millions of dollars so money isn't impressive. I've experienced some of the most direct racist remarks dealing with New York styled brokers-dealers. But I appreciate them for being direct, in my face, instead expressing their true feelings behind my back. This lets me know what kind of people I'm dealing with, and how I need to handle the situation. It's like having to make a deal with the devil. You know he doesn't like you, but he likes your company. You don't like him, but you have to deal with him to move forward. The racism is real at this level. And they don't have any issue letting know how they feel about you to your face. So it took some time to find a broker-dealer that would take my company on, just because I was black. Because I'm black, a lot of brokerage firms would turn the deal down. I never got offended, though. Now that I'm thinking about it, I should've been mad as hell. I just brush it off and keep going. I just don't have time to dwell on any kind of foolishness, even when it involves money.

But I wanted to tell you this story because you will experience some racism on your financing journey. You will need to learn how to handle that appropriately if there such a thing. It doesn't matter how well dressed you are, how much money you have, how great your company is, there are a lot of people and financial funds and institutions that just will not deal with you, solely because you're black. Remember, when you experience something like this because you will, don't get mad. Being mad takes to much of your precious time and energy that could otherwise go towards your funding efforts. The trick is, never let someone knock you to their level of ignorance.

They'll drag you down to their level and beat your ass.

You can never win a battle with someone else level that's beneath you. Sometimes the racism will be very subtle, but enough that you'll pick up on it.

This is why theurbanrapport.com was created. It's not only a black business directory, but it's a nesting site for all Black businesses to collaborate, network, share knowledge and information, and help uplift each other by working together. So you might have answers to some of my business questions, and I might have some answers to yours. By the both of us working together, by sharing knowledge and information, our businesses will flourish faster. Every business needs that group of shareholders that the owner can turn to in times of need. Rather its money, information, or technical insights you need a group to help you along your path. And that's what theurbanrapport.com is about.

So that's why it's crucial to always have your best foot forward when dealing with people who don't necessarily have your best interest at heart outside of making a dollar. Not only do you have to be sharp physically, but mentally sharp as well. If you're asking for a $1million dollars, you'll have to present yourself like you already have $1million dollars before they take you seriously. Always look like what you talk about. Be what comes out your mouth. Because you're African-American, you don't have the luxury of not being on point. Someone else could run a business in the ground, and people will say, "Oh that was just a learning experience for him. He'll get it back and be better the next time around." But when you do the same thing it's more like this, " Oh he wasn't ready. He should've known better." You have to continuously fight whatever stereotype these financiers have about black people. Always be the best presenter of yourself and your business that you can.

I encourage any black business to go this route because we need more black owned companies on wall street. That's why I personally have information posted at theurbranrapport.com to help you accomplish getting your business listed on the NYSE.

There aren't enough black VCs or broker-dealer firms in America, and we need more.

I have information on taking your company public in the member's section of **theurbanrapport.com**. You'll have the information that's needed to take your company public. You might find a better way for you other than taking your company public. That's what the urban rapport is about, helping you take your business to the next level.

Chapter Eight

Direct Public Offerings

"Ideas are meaningless without a masterful execution."
—Alejandro Cremades

Direct Public Offerings or DPOs (under the Regulation D section of the SEC code of regulations), allows you solicit investments for a private company, without the help of a broker-dealer. Most people know about IPOs (which stand for Initial Public Offerings), but A DPO is a Direct Public Offering. The main difference between the two is an IPO is a public offering, whereas a DPO is a private offering. Broker-dealers only deal with IPOs, which is making a company's shares available to the general public. A DPO only can solicit accredited investors to invest privately. The shares of a DPO will not be on the stock market like an IPO. You will need a track record to get a broker-dealer to list your company. A DPO is better suited for businesses raising funds to start operations. IPOs, you will need to already be operating.

With an IPO, you can be in business less than two years and have a broker-dealer list your company. The trick is you'll have to have your paperwork in order before you start operations. By law, broker-dealers will need to prove seasoning of investments on paper. This legitimizes the business in the eyes of the SEC. Then the brokerage firm will manage the IPO process from beginning to end. But with DPO, you'll have to create the fundraising campaign yourself. How do you do this? Easy, let me explain.

First, you'll need to hire someone to create a professional PPM (which is a private placement memorandum). A PPM is a professional investment document that describes all your business plans, and risk associated with your investment. This document will need to be submitted to the SEC and National Edgars Filing system, along with applicable state fees for each state you plan on raising funds in. The easiest way to get a PPM created and submitted is to hire a securities attorney. They will prepare the document and submit it for approval to all government agencies.

In my personal experience, I've spent $10k on just the PPM(private placement memorandum) For my real estate sourcing company. Along with the cost of the PPM, you'll have state fees to pay so you can raise capital in different states. These costs can range from $150-$400 per state! On top of that, you will want to hire a professional fundraiser to reach the accredited investors.

Because only those deemed as an accredited investor, by the government, will be allowed to invest in your company through a DPO. The fundraiser's job is to find these accredited investors, and present them your PPM. Fundraisers cost are based on how many people will be working your campaign on an hourly basis. This is a weekly expense. Then you'll have another cost like printing manuals and information guides that you'll have to send to investors.

A DPO offering is the most expensive way to raise capital, but it's one the easiest ways to raise millions of dollars by yourself. You have full control over the entire process. From of the amount of the investment to the terms of the money. If an investor agrees and chooses to subscribe, then he or she will pay you directly instead of going through a broker. So you will need a CPA to make sure you're on par with all government regulations.

Even though this is the most expensive way to raise money, it's well worth it. Because you'll have access to all the capital you need, and then some on your terms. And if you lose the money, there's no recourse banks, angels, and VCs. You're in control of your destiny. DPOs are a tremendous tool for business expansions. Because you can raise any amount of money, you wish. So if you're not intending on doing some major expanding, then this isn't for you. But if you are, then this is it. There is step by step free information at theurbanrapport.com, use the information at will.

A few things I want to add to this. When you decide on going the DPO route, make sure you have more than enough money set aside. Because you'll have to pay attorneys, CPAs, fundraisers, handle printing cost, and many more cost. You'll have to have a marketing plan done and worked by a marketer to raise awareness. Lately, there are several very resourceful websites that will allow you to place your PPM up for investors to view. You can expect a good 6-12 months to complete your first round of financing. Just make sure you have people who are experienced working your campaign. Don't hire an attorney who knows nothing about securities law. Or a tax specialist who only does seasonal taxes. You'll need experienced professionals at your disposal.

You'll need a great fundraiser. Once you have everything done and filed with Edgars, and get your Edgars number, you might start getting calls from people who wanting to raise the funds for you. This is okay, but you cannot pay them a percentage of any kind. You'll have to pay them a flat fee, up front, regardless of the outcome. The SEC made it illegal for you to pay someone based on their results in raising your funds. This is because they could be considered financial brokers, for which they're not. So you'll have to be careful when dealing with these fundraisers. Because if they don't follow the SEC's rules, then you and them might be going to jail for securities fraud. So make sure you check the fundraiser's credentials and references thoroughly. And if you get one doubt about the fundraiser, move on to the next. Follow your intuition at all times when your at this level in the game. You can find detailed information at theurbanrapport.com

Real Life Situation

Ok so after the venture capitalist deal fell through. I decided to go the DPO route before I found a broker-dealer. I hired a company to do my PPM, Edgars, and all my state filings.

After I had received the PPM, I had to search for a reputable fundraising company. It took me months to find a credible fundraiser. But when I did find a fundraiser, we got down to business fast. Within two weeks after signing the agreement, the fundraising campaign was live. The first week, we had some potential investors. After going back and forth a few times, we managed to strike a few deals. This was something completely new to me, and I had to learn on the fly. But all in all, the campaign was a success. And I can always do another one now that I have one under my belt. The second round should be much easier now if I chose to go that route again.

But the main cost that caught me off guard was the printing cost. You would think people nowadays are using email for business related communications. But I found that not to be true. Most of my investors wanted a the PPM in hand so they could hold and read. Printing each PPM cost me $100 bucks, not including the overnight shipping which ran about $25 dollars each PPM sent. So if you run your fundraising campaign correctly, and end up with 10 leads. That's $1,250 just for printing and shipping. From those ten PPMs that went out, you might close one or two deals. So you can see very well why the DPO route is one of the most expensive financing routes to take.

Along with the printing cost, you'll still have fundraisers to pay. These people charge by the hour per person. Each person working your campaign gets an hourly wage regardless how many leads they produce, you'll still have to pay this fee. When I first started out, I was paying $1,500 a week to the two people working my campaign. You can see very well why this route is the most expensive. But look if you can afford it, the land is yours to take. You can raise any amount of money you wish, and that's the good thing about the DPO route.

Hands down this is my favorite financing route to take because of the control it offers. I have complete control of everything, and I have the power to turn down subscriptions if I wanted to. And I can set how much the subscription buy-in will be.

I would recommend the DPO route to anybody who can afford it. And if you can't afford running your own DPO. Make it your goal to be able to do so.

There's a lot of resources for those who are thinking about running your own DPO at theurbanrapport.com. You'll be able to put everything together using the information that we have posted up.

Chapter Nine
Crowd Based Funding

"The value of an idea lies in the use of it." —Thomas Edison

Crowdbased funding is something that's been around for only 10 years or so. This is a social platform where average people can contribute small amounts of money to your business. Hundreds of people will end up funding your business efforts at an interest rate set by you. But to be competitive, you'll need to set the interest rates slightly above prime, which is the bank's going rate.

Crowdfunding is great when you need a longer financing term at a better interest rate than hard money or revenue based loans. There're several crowdfunding sites out there. Some sites have credit requirements, but most don't. You'll have to submit a traditional banking loan app called 1003, and applicable tax information to qualify to present your offering to a crowd. On top of that, some individuals will want further information from you before contributing to the investment. There's good and bad in this. The good thing is, you're not dealing with a bank, and you can set your own terms. The bad thing is you'll be dealing with hundreds of individual investors who might want individualized information from you. Someone might want further tax information, someone else might want specific business information. This could be a daunting task trying to meet all the individualized request.

Crowdfunding works like so. Say there's a pool of 5000 people who are seeking higher interest rates than what banks are offering. You come along needing $2500. You submit your documents including your professional business plan with projections on a crowdfunding platform. Let's say half of the group sees your request and decides to fund it. So you will end up with 2500 people contributing small amounts to you. You set the terms, interest rates, and payment dates. On those dates, the payment amount will be deducted automatically from your bank account.

Once your loan is paid back, you'll be able to ask those same 2500 people for more money if you need to.

Investors like crowdfunding platforms because they can invest in high-risk companies without the risk. Because of all the people who contributed to your funding efforts share in the risk collectively.

So crowdfunding is something new and exciting. You can get some solid results going this route. We have a lot of resources for those who want to go the crowdfunding route at theurbanrapport.com.

The downside to crowdfunding is the time involved. It might take you more than a year to raise that $2500 depending on how good your proposal is. The investors will nickel and dime you to death. So it's a slow and tedious process. Crowdfunding requires patience.

One thing I do like about crowdfunding the investors will not know your nationality. I hate to put this in here, but it's the truth. If I told you different, then I'll be lying. So with these investors not knowing your African American the playing field is level. And when compared to other routes of funding, you might be surprised be getting funded faster. Whereas another funding avenue will know your nationality and might drag the process on, like at a bank.

But there are costs associated with this method of financing. You'll have to join the online crowdfunding platforms, which can cost around $300 a month. These are the platforms that you'll be submitting your PPM and business plan to for investors to view. So you can imagine how expensive this can get when you're campaigning on multiple sites at the same time to reach your funding goal.

Real Life Situations

I knew a woman that wanted a bagel shop. The lady talked about this dream store all the time. I believed she wanted me to invest at one point, but I had no interest in such a business endeavor. She came to class one day and started talking about she found the money for the shop. I was shocked. I wanted to know who in their right gave her some investment money when she had no knowledge or expertise in the field. So I had to ask to see if she was lying. She told me that she got the money through crowdfunding. I immediately went on a quest to find out about this new funding channel. I researched and researched and found everything I could about the subject. I even promoted a few small campaigns myself to see if it worked. And I quickly found out that crowdfunding really works.

With crowdfunding, you'll need to keep everything simple. Your documents should be so simple a 5th grader should be able to understand. You'll need to bear in mind that people who are on the platform are average everyday people, not businessmen and women. These people don't know all the technical jargon language that the bankers require. The average person will need to understand each and everything about your business. If you submit documents that are hard to comprehend, the potential investors will just pass on your business plan because not understand it.

So when you're going the crowdfunding route, make sure your docs are simple. Your docs don't have to be professionally done. Remember you want to speak the language of whoever you're trying to get money from.

Conclusion

Conclusion

Before we conclude this book, let me go over a couple things that may help you on your journey. There are a couple things you'll need to make sure is in order before you seek financing.

1. You Need To Be The Part.

Remember your African American and there's always a stereotype you'll have to fight. The further you are from that stereotype the better the chances of you getting funded. There's no room for error when asking for money. Present yourself in a business savvy manner. If you're trying to get funded, then make sure you look like it.

2. Know What You're Talking About.

By now you should have a business plan or plan on having one. Make sure you know that business plan like the back of your hand. You need to know every detail of that document. You're the authority on your business, and it needs to show.

You'll be amazed at how many people don't know what they really want. They'll take a wild guess, and then apply for financing. And when the financier starts asking specific questions, they'll come off as an amateur. This is because they don't really know what they're talking about. You have to remember, these lenders are professionals and like to deal with professionals. So they'll see BS a mile away. You cannot afford not to have your stuff together when in front of someone who's deciding on giving you money. Make sure your branding message, and business plan is together before seeking financing.

Always remember, it's not the destination, it's the journey!

Acknowledgments

SEJJ JACKSON

I'm going to make this short and sweet because I have too many friends and family that'll have to name all at once.

I want to thank the staff at The Urban Rapport for taking a chance on me. And believing in me and my work even during a time i didn't.

Let me say thank you to Ms. Marquette Chapman, for copywriting this book even during a funeral. Talking about dedication and belief. Its people like you that make me go hard everyday.

I have to tell my mother Ms. Tiffany Ivory that I love her dearly. And if it wasn't for your sacrifices, I wouldn't be the man you designed me to be.

To my pops, as much as I've tried not to be like you. I ended up just like you. Spittin image. Love you dearly, and keep being my example.

To all my brothers: Ishmael, Emmanuel, Malachi, and Arrik I love ya'll dearly. And hopefully I've been a great example for you.

I could go on and on for a few days. Thank you everybody..and if I didn't mention your name, just know its limited paper here to complete this book. And take this paragraph as me saying thank you so much.

About The Author

Purchasing his first real estate property at 17yrs old, and being coming a millionaire at by 18, now 30, Sejj Jackson has joined the league of one of the country's youngest successful real estates entrepreneurs by large. By being involved with some 3000 properties throughout his 13yrs of buying and selling real estate, Sejj Jackson has been acknowledged as one of the youngest property Titans in the game.

People have clamored to hear this young man speak during the very few speaking engagements he's agreed to do in the past 13yrs. Believing having his privacy, he's turned down countless speaking opportunities until now. He's grown to become one of the most sought after real estate titans in the country. With captivating stories that surround this man, like him turning $5,000 into a million dollar a year business in two years, make people want to know this man.

Sejj Jackson lives in Birmingham, AL but, has businesses that reach six different states. He has two pit bulls that he loves dearly. No kids, and likes to travel. He was diagnosed with Crohn's disease in May of 2016.

He credits his newly discovered illness for wanting to give the world his gift, which he says is the gift of making money.

You can catch him at:
www.mrsejj.com
www.theurbanrapport.com
Twitter/Mr.Sejj
Facebook/Sejj Jackson

www.ingramcontent.com/pod-product-compliance
Lightning Source LLC
Chambersburg PA
CBHW060403190526
45169CB00002B/735